smoothies

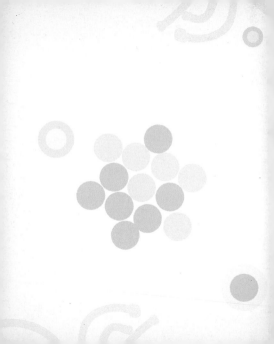

little books for cooks

Smoothies

Jane Stacey

Andrews McMeel
Publishing

Kansas City

Andrews McMeel Publishing
an Andrews McMeel Universal company
4520 Main Street
Kansas City, Missouri 64111

ISBN: 0-7407-0522-9

Library of Congress Catalog Card Number:
99-65534

First U.S. Edition
1 2 3 4 5 6 7 8 9 10

Editor: Deri Reed
Designer: Debra Sfetsios
Illustrator: John Hershey

Produced by Smallwood & Stewart, Inc.
New York City

contents

SMOO

introduction

dust off the blender, dig into your produce drawer, and jump into the world of smoothies. These wonderful, slushy drinks are easy to make,

thies

instantly refreshing, and always delicious. Whether you buzz up a quick batch for a breakfast on the run, a pick-me-up after a workout, or a fun, healthy snack for the kids, you'll soon discover that smoothies are perfect for today's fast-paced, healthy lifestyle.

Smoothies are loaded with fruit and vegetables, and it's no *new* news that eating a variety of fresh produce is good for us, adding the fiber, vitamins, and minerals that are essential for keeping us healthy and fit. Smoothies take advantage of the natural sweetness of fruit, satisfying the sweet tooth in us all. With such healthful thickeners as bananas and yogurt, smoothies are the perfect nutritional snack-in-a-glass. (Though the occasional scoop of frozen confection provides a nice indulgence.)

the great thing about smoothies

is that they can be whatever you want,

whenever you want. Hankering for melon at midnight? Throw some watermelon cubes in the blender along with ice, lime juice, and sugar and you have Strictly Watermelon. Need a caffeine fix at six A.M.? A Taste of East India, with black tea, milk, honey, and spices, will give you a wake-up call.

Smoothies for every mood are covered in this book, from fun fruity classics and nutrient-packed veggie blends to healthful exotic concoctions and decidedly decadent dessert medleys. And, keep in mind that smoothie recipes are very forgiving and practically beg for variations. So if one type of fruit isn't available in your area or you'd just like to try another (using nectarines instead of peaches, for example, or blackberries instead of raspberries), there's nothing to stop you from substituting freely. You say you don't care for nonfat yogurt? It's quite all right to use low-fat, or the full-fat variety, if you choose.

and whether you consider your-self an accomplished cook or rarely set foot in the kitchen, smoothies can be a great way to explore different flavor combinations. The important thing to remember is that smoothies are quick, fun, and healthy. So relax and enjoy, because

Smoothies are for everyone!

apricots

High in potassium and vitamin A (which
helps our bodies fight infection), fresh
apricots are usually only available in the
summer months. Look for plump, firm
fruit with no bruises; store at room
temperature until ripe.

bananas

A banana is at the heart of many
smoothies, acting as binder and thickener.

Though not essential in most smoothie recipes, if you use a frozen banana, you'll get a thicker, creamier slurp. To freeze, peel and slice the banana and place in a resealable freezer bag; freeze for up to three months.

blueberries

With respectable amounts of fiber and potassium, blueberries are a healthful ingredient in any smoothie. They freeze beautifully, and frozen berries will help thicken a smoothie (commercially frozen berries work well too).

brewer's yeast

Traditionally used for fermentation in beer-making, brewer's yeast is also used as a nutritional supplement, providing protein, B vitamins, minerals, and amino acids. Add one or two teaspoons to any smoothie for a nutritional boost.

carrot juice

Loaded with vitamin A (one cup has more than six times an adult's RDA) and, of course, beta carotene, carrot juice has become the darling of the health-food set. If you don't have a juice bar nearby, check the refrigerated juice section of your grocery store.

cherries

You can't beat a handful of cherries for adding color and tang to a smoothie. Be sure to pit cherries before whirling them in the blender. For the best texture, pit fresh cherries and freeze them ahead of time (in resealable plastic bags).

ginger

For centuries, this pungent spice with a peppery, almost-sweet bite has been settling upset stomachs. Recent research indicates that it also helps relieve muscle aches and arthritis pain. Fresh ginger is usually found in the produce section of larger grocery stores; look for plump solid roots with smooth, unwrinkled skin. Use a vegetable peeler to peel away ginger's tough skin, then grate with a small-holed grater

kiwis

Considered by some to be New Zealand's finest gift to the Northern Hemisphere, kiwis are small, brown-skinned fruit with emerald green, sweet, buttery flesh. They have the best flavor when they are slightly soft to the touch. Allow to ripen at room temperature, then remove the peel with a knife.

Mangoes

Loaded with beta carotene and vitamin C, mangoes add a sweet, peachy, slightly exotic flavor to smoothies. Look for unblemished skins that feel slightly tender when touched. It's easiest to cut around the mango's large stubborn pit rather than pulling it out with your fingers. When fresh mango is unavailable, mango slices in a jar (in the refrigerated section of your produce department) are a good alternative.

Milk

The recipes in this book were developed using 2 percent milk, but there's no reason you can't use whole or nonfat milk, if you like. Nondairy alternatives could also be used: Soy milk, made from cooked soybeans, is rich in iron and protein; rice milk, pressed from brown rice, is usually fortified with calcium and vitamins A and D. Be aware, however, that using soy milk or rice milk will change the flavor of the smoothie.

papayas

Not quite as exotic as they used to be, these sweet-but-slightly-tart tropical fruits are usually available in gourmet markets and large supermarkets. Cut in half and scoop out the bitter seeds before peeling and chopping.

Sherbet, Sorbet

There seems to be much confusion about sherbet and sorbet. Sorbet is the easier:

It's like a smooth ice or granita, consisting of fruit juice that has been sweetened, then processed like ice cream. Sherbet is made from sweetened fruit juice as well, but with milk added for a bit of richness.

wheat germ

The heart of wheat kernels, wheat germ is a good source of fiber, protein, vitamin E, B vitamins, and iron. Add a tablespoon or two to a smoothie for a fiber boost.

yogurt

Besides bananas, yogurt is one of the more popular thickeners used in smoothies. In these recipes, we will sometimes specify the type of yogurt (nonfat, low-fat, etc.), but feel free to follow your dietary needs and use whichever kind you prefer, including nondairy soy-based yogurt. Check the label for "live cultures" or "active cultures," which indicates the presence of acidophilus, beneficial bacteria that help keep your digestive system in good health.

basic

smoothies

Strawberry royale

Satisfying and not too sweet, this is the queen bee of all smoothies. Bananas and ice make it thick, orange juice adds sweetness, and yogurt brings a pleasing creaminess. It's perfect first thing in the morning.

- 1½ **cups sliced fresh strawberries**
- 1 **ripe banana, sliced**
- 3 **ice cubes**
- ½ **cup plain yogurt (nonfat or low-fat)**
- ¼ **cup orange juice**

Place the straw-berries, banana, and ice in a blender and pulse 3 or 4 times. Add the yogurt and orange juice. Blend until smooth.

Serves 2.

Strawberry Punch

For a nutritional power punch, add 1 tablespoon wheat germ or 1 to 2 tea-spoons nutritional or brewer's yeast.

peachy treat

Peaches from the backyard
(sliced, then frozen) or store-bought
frozen peaches work equally well in
this smoothie. The honey contributes
sweetness and depth, while the ginger
adds a subtle, peppery bite.

- 1½ **cups frozen peach slices (from about 2 fresh peaches)**
- ½ **cup orange juice**
- ½ **cup vanilla or peach yogurt (nonfat, low-fat, or whole-milk)**
- 1 **tablespoon honey**
- 1 **teaspoon freshly grated peeled ginger**

Place the peaches and orange juice in a blender and pulse until a chunky mixture forms. Add the yogurt, honey, and ginger and blend until smooth. *serves 2.*

peachy protein treat

For a nondairy smoothie with a burst of protein, substitute ½ cup chilled soft silken tofu for the yogurt and increase the honey to taste.

black 'N' blueberry

a touch of lemon heightens the berry flavors in this vibrant magenta smoothie. If you are using fresh berries and want a thicker smoothie, add an ice cube or two when blending the berries and yogurt.

- **³/₄ cup frozen or fresh blackberries**
- **³/₄ cup frozen or fresh blueberries**
- **³/₄ cup vanilla, blueberry, or plain yogurt**
- **½ cup grape juice**
- **1 teaspoon fresh lemon juice**
- **¼ cup milk**

Place the blackberries, blueberries, and yogurt in a blender and blend until a chunky mixture forms. Add the grape juice and lemon juice and blend. Add the milk and blend until smooth.

Serves 2.

cranberry zipper

the zippy red color of this smoothie is as refreshing as its flavor. The applesauce gives just the right touch of sweetness without affecting the texture.

- 1 **cup fresh or frozen raspberries**
- ½ **cup fresh cranberries or canned cranberry sauce**
- 3 **ice cubes**
- ½ **cup applesauce**
- ½ **cup cranberry juice**

Place the raspberries and cranberries in a blender and pulse until a chunky mixture forms. Add the ice and blend. Add the applesauce and cranberry juice and blend until smooth. *serves* 2.

raspberry slip

the heavenly combination of luscious red raspberries and creamy yogurt can't be beat. And it is healthy, too, because raspberries contain surprising amounts of iron, potassium, and vitamins A and D.

$1^3/_4$ **cups fresh or frozen raspberries**

1 **cup vanilla, raspberry, or plain yogurt**

$^1/_2$ **cup milk**

2 **tablespoons frozen white grape juice or orange juice concentrate**

Place all the ingredients in a blender and blend until smooth. *serves 2.*

blackberry slip
If blackberries are available, use instead of raspberries for equally delicious results.

autumn
spicy icy

pears, naturally quite sweet, blend well with the traditional pumpkin pie flavors of maple, cinnamon, allspice, and cloves. Find an especially ripe pear for this smoothie—or allow one to ripen for a few days outside the refrigerator. The flesh should yield easily, especially around the stem.

1   ripe pear, peeled, cored, and quartered
1   banana, sliced
2   ice cubes
1   cup maple yogurt
⅛   teaspoon pumpkin pie spice

In a blender, combine the pear, banana, and ice cubes. Pulse until a chunky mixture forms. Add the yogurt and pumpkin pie spice and blend until smooth. *serves 2.*

Healthful add-in
For a smoothie with added fiber, add 1 tablespoon wheat or oat bran with the yogurt and pumpkin pie spice and blend until smooth.

cherry-o

Cherry-blossom pink and simply divine tasting, this smoothie matches frozen cherries and cherry yogurt with the delicate sweetness of pear. Fresh cherries, available from May or June through August, make a scrumptious smoothie as well.

1   **cup frozen pitted dark cherries**

½   **pear, peeled, cored, and quartered**

3   **ice cubes**

1   **cup cherry-vanilla yogurt or 1 cup cherry yogurt plus ½ teaspoon vanilla extract**

½   **cup milk or cherry juice**
⅛   **teaspoon almond extract**

Place the cherries, pear, and ice cubes in a blender and pulse until a chunky mixture forms. Add the yogurt, milk, and almond extract and blend until smooth. *serves 2.*

triple-citrus squeeze

thirst quenching on even the most scorching summer days, this fizzy smoothie combines lemon, lime, and orange with the power of ginseng, a root that has been cultivated for centuries in China for its restorative properties. Ginseng soda can be found in many natural-food stores. Ginger ale is a fine substitute.

- ¼ **cup fresh lemon juice**
- ¼ **cup fresh lime juice**
- ¼ **cup fresh orange juice**
- 4 **ice cubes**
- 1 **cup ginseng soda or ginger ale**

Combine the lemon juice, lime juice, orange juice, and ice cubes in a blender. Blend until a slushy mixture forms. Add the ginseng soda and pulse briefly, just until frothy. Pour into two ice-filled glasses. *serves* **2.**

strictly
watermelon

●asy as 1-2-3 and super refreshing after a trip to the pool or the beach. This is a great way to use that last wedge of watermelon wrapped in the fridge.

4 **cups seeded watermelon cubes**

4 **ice cubes**

1 **tablespoon fresh lime juice**

1 **tablespoon sugar**

Place 2 cups of
the watermelon and
the ice cubes
in a blender
and pulse
until a chunky
mixture forms. Add
the remaining 2 cups
of watermelon,
the lime juice,
and sugar
and blend until frothy.
serves 2.

the good old summertime

Peaches and raspberries blend up beautifully for this refreshing, summery treat. This is also a good way to enjoy the taste of summer the whole year long; just remember to freeze some fruit during the dog days.

- **1 cup frozen peach slices (from 1 large peach)**
- **½ cup frozen or fresh raspberries**
- **½ banana**
- **½ cup orange juice or milk**

Place all the ingredients in a blender and blend until smooth. *serves 2.*

cherry fizz

*S*erve this tasty combo in old-fashioned punch cups at a preteen party. Watch out though—grown-ups like it too!

1   cup frozen pitted dark cherries

5   ice cubes

1/2   cup Cherry 7-Up or regular 7-Up

Place the cherries and ice cubes in a blender and pulse until a slushy mixture forms. Add the 7-Up and blend just until smooth.

serves 2.

good
Morning

*S*tart your day off right with this
flavorful smoothie. It blends
up thick and rich—and
satisfying enough for a
breakfast on the run.

1 frozen sliced banana

¼ ripe cantaloupe, cubed (about 1 cup)

½ cup frozen strawberries

½ cup orange juice

Place all the ingredients in a blender and blend until smooth. **Serves 2.**

Minty Morning Add 2 or 3 coarsely chopped fresh mint leaves before blending.

Peachy Morning Substitute 1 cup frozen peach slices for the banana.

Maple Morning Add ½ cup maple yogurt before blending.

veggie

smoothies

carrot-apple jazz

Even if you've never been a fan of carrot juice, try this delicious icy concoction. The bold flavor of carrot juice is mellowed by sweet apple juice and creamy yogurt.

46

- 5 ice cubes
- ½ cup plain yogurt (nonfat or low-fat)
- 3 tablespoons frozen apple juice concentrate
- ¾ cup carrot juice
- ½ teaspoon freshly grated ginger or ¼ teaspoon ground ginger

Place the ice cubes in a blender and pulse until partially crushed. Add the yogurt and apple juice concentrate and blend until thick and almost smooth. Add the carrot juice and ginger and blend again briefly, just until smooth.

serves 2.

cucumber cooler

this could be lunch on a hot summer day with a side serving of crisp rye crackers. Or try it as an appetizer before a light supper off the grill. If your cucumber is especially seedy, halve it lengthwise and use a spoon to scoop out the seeds before slicing. If you like, add sour cream for a touch of richness and lemon juice to brighten the flavor.

2   cups peeled sliced cucumber
    (from about 2 small cucumbers)
3   ice cubes
½   cup buttermilk
1   teaspoon chopped fresh parsley
½   teaspoon chopped fresh mint
1   tablespoon sour cream (optional)
1   teaspoon lemon juice (optional)

Place the cucumber and ice cubes in the blender and pulse until a chunky mixture forms. Add the buttermilk, parsley, mint, and sour cream and lemon juice, if using; blend until frothy. **serves 2.**

icy Hot tomato

A wild blend of carrot juice, fresh tomato, and a dash of your favorite hot sauce makes this a spicy veggie blast. Serve in small glasses as a healthful pick-me-up late in the afternoon or as a low-calorie aperitif before dinner.

- **1 cup chopped fresh tomato**
- **3 ice cubes**
- **¾ cup carrot juice**
- **2 teaspoons hot sauce, or to taste**
- **¼ teaspoon chopped fresh dill**

Place the tomato and ice in a blender and pulse until a chunky mixture forms. Add the carrot juice, hot sauce, and dill and blend until frothy. **serves 2.**

exotic

smoothies

HONEYdEW'LL do it!

the juicy end-of-summer sweetness of ripe honeydew melon combines with tangy lime sherbet for this cool, refreshing slurp.

- **2 cups cubed honeydew melon**
- **½ cup lime sherbet**
- **3 tablespoons lime juice**
- **1 teaspoon coarsely chopped fresh mint leaves (optional)**

Place the melon, sherbet, and lime juice in a blender and blend until smooth. Add the mint leaves, if using, and pulse quickly once or twice, just to combine. **serves 2.**

Mango-apricot Magic

Early summer, when fresh apricots are readily available, is the time to indulge in this blissfully delicious dessert-style smoothie.

- **1 cup cubed mango**
- **1 cup chopped fresh apricots**
- **1 cup apricot nectar**
- **¾ cup tangerine frozen yogurt, orange sherbet, or orange sorbet**

Place all the ingredients in a blender and blend until smooth. *Serves 2.*

papa-pineapple breeze

Lose yourself in the tropics with this humdinger blend of fresh papaya, pineapple, and coconut. Papaya contains a special enzyme that is known to be beneficial to digestion.

- 1½ **cups cubed fresh papaya**
- ½ **cup canned crushed pineapple**
- ½ **cup light coconut milk**
- ½ **cup orange juice**

Place all the ingredients in a blender and blend until smooth. *serves 2.*

kiNder colada

the traditional piña colada is a cold, creamy combination of rum, ice, pineapple, and cream of coconut. We've lightened it by substituting coconut milk and frozen yogurt for the rich cream of coconut. A banana adds body and creaminess. A shot of rum is a fine addition, if you're so inclined.

- 1 banana, sliced
- ³/₄ cup pineapple chunks
- ³/₄ cup light coconut milk
- ³/₄ cup vanilla frozen yogurt

Place all the ingredients in a blender and blend until smooth. *serves 2.*

tropical passion

passion fruit can be difficult to seed and not always readily available; an easily accessible source of its exotic taste is passion fruit nectar and sorbet. Here is a triple dose of the tropics with passion fruit nectar and sorbet blended with pineapple and banana.

- **1 banana, sliced**
- **1½ cups passion fruit sorbet**
- **¾ cup passion fruit nectar or juice**
- **¼ cup canned crushed pineapple**

Place the banana and sorbet in a blender and pulse until chunky. Add the juice and pineapple and blend until smooth. **serves 2.**

MaNgo Moo

the fabulous buttery flavor of ripe mango is what this smoothie is all about. Just a touch of heavy cream makes for velvety perfection.

1½ **cups peeled diced mango (from about 1 large mango)**

1   **cup mango sorbet**

¼   **cup orange juice**

¼   **cup heavy cream**

1   **tablespoon fresh lemon juice**

Place the mango, mango sorbet, orange juice, and cream in a blender and blend until smooth. Add the lemon juice and blend again briefly, just to combine.
serves 2.

kiwi COMMOTION

Once kiwis were quite an exotic fruit, grown in New Zealand and available only seasonally. Now they are grown in California and show up in our supermarkets year-round. Since the tiny black seeds inside the kiwi become bitter when they are overblended, use a food processor; it doesn't seem to crush the seeds as much as a blender.

2 **kiwis, peeled and quartered**

1 **banana, sliced**

³/₄ **cup vanilla frozen yogurt (nonfat or low-fat)**

¹/₄ **cup frozen limeade concentrate**

Place the kiwis, banana, and frozen yogurt in a food processor and pulse 3 or 4 times Add the limeade concentrate and process just until smooth.

serves 2.

taste of east india

Energize your morning or afternoon
with this pungent and flavorful blend of
black tea, bananas, and spices.
Cardamom, an aromatic spice with a
distinctive aroma, is available finely
ground or whole. If you have whole
seeds, use a mortar and pestle to grind
them and use just a pinch.

1½ **frozen sliced bananas**

3 **ice cubes**

½ **cup strongly brewed black tea,
cooled to room temperature**

⅓ **cup milk**

    1   **tablespoon honey**
   1/8 **teaspoon ground cardamom**
   1/8 **teaspoon ground cinnamon**

Place the banana and ice cubes in a blender and blend until a chunky mixture forms. Add the tea, milk, honey, cardamom, and cinnamon and blend until smooth. *serves 2.*

pink shirley

Perfumed and pink, this smoothie is an elegant, almost-grown-up treat for a little girl's birthday party. Pour into tall parfait glasses and garnish with tiny paper umbrellas. If you can't find passion fruit or guava spritzer, plain old strawberry spritzer will do nicely. For the best taste, look for spritzers that contain real fruit puree rather than artificial flavors.

- 1 **cup sliced fresh strawberries**
- 1 **cup strawberry sorbet**
- 2 **tablespoons sour cream**
- ½ **cup guava or passion fruit spritzer**

Place the strawberries, strawberry sorbet, and sour cream in a blender and blend until almost smooth. Add the spritzer and blend again briefly, just until well blended and frothy. **serves 2.**

java 'N' love

Indulgent and seductively sweet, but with a punch of espresso power, this smoothie is guaranteed to satisfy all your cravings. Share this with someone you love after a romantic dinner.

- 1½ **cups chocolate caramel ice cream or your favorite chocolate-based ice cream**
- 1 **sliced banana**
- ¾ **cup milk**
- ¼ **cup espresso, cooled to room temperature**
- ⅛ **teaspoon ground cinnamon**

Place all the ingredients in a blender and blend until smooth. **ſerveſ 2.**

p.b. jolt Substitute 2 tablespoons peanut butter for the banana and add 2 ice cubes.

berry jolt Substitute 1 cup frozen raspberries or strawberries for the banana and decrease the milk to ½ cup.

blue Moon

Perfect for a hot summer night under a full moon, this slushy concoction is refreshing and not too sweet. Blue curaçao, like orange curaçao, is a sweet orange-flavored liqueur made from the peel of bitter oranges that first grew on the Caribbean island of Curaçao. Enjoy one without the vodka, too.

- 2/3 **cup lemon sorbet**
- 2 **ice cubes**
- 1/2 **cup lemonade**
- 1/4 **cup citrus-flavored vodka**
- 2 **teaspoons blue curaçao**

Place the sorbet, ice cubes, lemonade, and vodka in a blender and pulse just until smooth. Pour into two frozen martini glasses. Use a spoon to dot the surface of each smoothie in several places with blue curaçao. Then use a toothpick to swirl the blue curaçao into spirals. Alternately, stir the blue curaçao into the smoothie to create a minty green color. **serves 2.**

creamsicle dream

remember those paddle-shaped orange popsicles with creamy vanilla ice cream inside? At the park, at night, in the summer? This smoothie brings it all back—but less sticky. For a grown-up exotic version, try it with pistachio ice cream and top it with chopped pistachios and tiny chocolate chips.

1½ **cups vanilla ice cream**

1 **cup mandarin orange sections, fresh or canned**

½ **cup heavy cream or milk**

2 **tablespoons frozen orange juice concentrate**

1 **teaspoon vanilla extract**

Place all the ingredients in a blender and blend until smooth. *serves 2.*

cheers

this smoothie is a close relative to two other champagne drinks, the Mimosa, which combines champagne and orange juice, and the Bellini, which uses peach puree. It's a delight-ful addition to a Sunday brunch or birthday luncheon celebration. If you want to make a large batch for a party, first whiz up the peaches and orange juice separately, then add the champagne and pulse briefly to combine. As with all champagne drinks, serve immediately.

1 **cup frozen or fresh peach slices, chopped**

½ **cup orange juice**

¾ **cup champagne**

Place all the ingredients in a blender and blend just until smooth.
Serves 2.

Mud pie

Looks aren't everything, as this chocolaty muddle proves. The flecks of chocolate sandwich cookies are guaranteed to bring you right back to the days of after-school snacks.

- **1 frozen sliced banana**
- **½ cup chocolate milk**
- **3 chocolate sandwich cookies (such as Oreos), crumbled**
- **¼ teaspoon vanilla extract**

Place all the ingredients in a blender and blend until smooth. *Serves 2.*

Mocha Mud Pie Add ¼ cup coffee.

p.b. & Mud Pie Add 2 tablespoons peanut butter.

Minty Mud Pie Substitute chocolate mint cookies (such as Mint Milanos) for the chocolate sandwich cookies.

Gourmet Mud Pie Add 2 ounces chopped top-quality semisweet chocolate (such as Valrhona, Lindt, or Ghirardelli).

illustrations by john hershey